Inspirational Spa: From the Womb of the Morning

A Spa Treatment of Poems

Nettie Millard

ISBN: 150036097X

ISBN 13: 9781500360979

Library of Congress Control Number: 2014911951

CreateSpace Independent Publishing Platform

North Charleston, South Carolina

To my lovely mother, beautiful sisters and amazing brother: From the womb of the morning, your love and support are indelible.

To God only wise, be glory. Thank you to Diane, Demaune, Terrylynn, Helen and Denise. Your candid review and feedback were invaluable. Thanks for your inspirational spa treatment of good times, good food and good fun. Lavon, you too will always have a special place in my heart.

In loving memory of:

my father
Harry A. Millard
Handsome, strong and consummate provider

great-aunt
Pyocinese Anderson
Beautiful, stylish and tremendous encourager

and

great-grandfather
Ferdinand Doughty
Scholar, educator and preacher

The Author To The Reader

❦

Dear Reader,

The soul of day rests in the darkness, in seeming obscurity. Yet out of the darkness, the sun emerges from beneath the horizon as subtly and steadily as it returns. Like the genesis of a masterpiece, the day dawns from the womb of the morning; a matrix that protects, develops and births reality through every thought, word and deed to paint a world known and unknown with a resplendence often taken for granted.

In the starlight of morning, restoration and rejuvenation dutifully serves humankind to prepare, reflect, move forward, create, act and be; the essence of which is the ability to begin again, to start anew. There is a freshness, a particular newness, a nuanced purity indigenous to morning in that it is the prologue to another day; ushering that day into a natural existence without the assistance or approval of itself or any other creation. Therefore; even as the day, in all of its splendor and glory, needs no permission to be; neither do you. The difference however is that you have a choice.

Every day one can choose to dare celebrate life and love, face and overcome challenges, convert fear to faith, embrace hopes and realize dreams while hearing the unheard, seeing the unseen, speaking the unspoken and writing the unwritten; oftentimes unknowingly becoming an instrument of change while positively touching the lives of others along the way. Clothed with the night, morning morphs into a compass of daylight to help guide, interpret and traverse this wonderfully enigmatic state of being called life.

Understanding that day is merely night draped in light; a bird sings its early morning song as the dew evaporates and night yields to dawn to reveal a refreshing expectation of another day's journey. A journey marked by perennial untraveled moments in time that will not cease until eternity's cup is filled to overflowing with the manifestation of all of humanity's indwelling greatness.

Now dear reader, may you grow in grace, stand strong and forsake not the essence of yourself. May you enter each day from the womb of the morning; embracing life with a renewed sense of appreciation, expectation, anticipation and purpose. In the midst of impossibilities, may you see the possible. May you envision the end from the beginning and be ready to encourage yourself against all odds. If you feel stuck or blocked, reinvent yourself and chart another path.

Be cautious that flattering words enter not into your head and that disparaging words enter not into your heart for they are fleetingly toxic. Find and nurture rest for your soul. Render unto yourself mercy when you make mistakes and seek constructive and enduring change. Understand that perfection is not a position, rather a pursuit.

You were not created for the world; hence let it not define you. The world was created for you, so rise, shine and define your place. The universe awaits your alignment. Have a vision, be specific, else at the world's whim you are blown like a feather in its wind.

Periodic self-imposed solitude has its place for reflection, regeneration and recovery from the stressors of life. Be mindful however to cultivate relationships because prolonged seclusion may nourish sorrow and bitterness. True friends are known by their motivations; therefore discern who they are and cherish them; lest when they are gone, regret takes their place. Fellowship with like minds is a thorn in the flesh to envy and jealousy.

Share and guard time wisely for it leaves your legacy. If you are a receiver, learn to give. If you are a giver, learn to receive. Be balanced.

Inspirationally yours,

Nettie Millard

Contents

⮞⮜

Introduction

৵৽

Recently during a light early morning rain, I came upon a verse of scripture (Psalm 110:3) with the phrase, "from the womb of the morning." This phraseology struck me as interestingly profound and particularly poetic. Later that same morning, I took advantage of a Spa Getaway given to me as a birthday gift. The full body massage, hot stones and other spa treatments were invigorating to my body, stimulating to my senses and relaxing to my mind. That day, both the scripture and spa experience were refreshing and inspiring in a way not easily described.

Therefore, it will suffice to say that inspiration is comparable to discovering a hidden treasure that was always in plain sight; hidden by a translucent door of enlightenment. Once that door is opened and one enters, there is an awakening which results in a powerful revelation that expands one's reality. A reality upon which corresponding action must be taken. For me, that action translated into the compilation of this poetic work, *Inspirational Spa: From the Womb of the Morning - A Spa Treatment of Poems.*

With an imprint of culture and conscience, poetry and spas share the characteristic of providing deliberate or unplanned inspiration through relaxation or stimulation. As partners, they are rhythmically therapeutic to the mind, body and spirit. With that thinking in mind, this book of poems consists of recurring themes centered around God, time, eternity, destiny and self. It comprises poems I have written over the years, some of which were featured on my CD of Poetry entitled: Inspiraction (circa, 2002).

This book is segmented into four Inspirational Spa Treatments and they are:

I.   Resilient Full Body Massage – Poems which depict faith and resilience
II. Motivational Deep Tissue Massage – Energizing words of positive action
III. Appreciative Hot Stone Massage – Poetry written in admiration and celebration of various milestones in life
IV. Self-Reflective Facial – Poems of introspection

Whatever your belief, or lack thereof (unbelief is within itself a belief), my hope is that within these pages there will be a verse, phrase or even a word to serve as a source of encouragement or edification; if but for a moment, to see, realize and know the intangible power that resides on the inside of each of us to persevere and produce tangible results. Power is most often present when you press for the prize.

This book combines poetry with elements of self-provoking thought. As a result, at the end of each segment there is a Massage Therapy Pressure Point session with a corresponding Reflection Exercise to help you rewind, rethink, reassess, regroup, refresh and reset in order to be recharged to restart and regain a desired result.

And now beloved reader, the appointment is set for us to partake of this Inspirational Spa Treatment of Poems together.

INSPIRATIONAL SPA
TREATMENT I

꙳⚬꙳

RESILIENT FULL BODY
MASSAGE

throughout history
you have conquered fear
and have defied the odds
for all the world to see your victory

THE BEAT

I hear the sound of the beat
in the distance

the beat of joy, the beat of sorrow
the beat of yesterday, today and tomorrow

the beat of greatness, the beat of shame
the beat of victory, the beat of pain

the beat of dreams alive
the beat of dreams that dried

the beat of heaven, sea and earth
the beat of the universe

the beat of creation dancing to the Creator's song
the beat discerning right and wrong

the beat of laughter, the beat of crying
the beat of new birth, the beat of dying

the beat of war, the beat of peace
the beat of famine, the beat of feast

the beat of hate, the beat of love
the beat negotiating the human heart like a dove

the beat of my ancestors, my offspring, myself
the beat protecting freedom
from enslavement's shelf

the beat of the impossible
conquered by the possible
is the beat I hear
from generation to generation
from year to year

eternity has opened its ear
and moves to the beat
without time, within time, beyond time

rejecting the beat unknown
reflecting the beat of its own sound
its own rhythm
its own music
its own song
its own word
its own silence

filled with its own faith
clothed with its own purpose
embedded in its own people

who live, breathe, taste, see
hear, feel, sense and know
the beat of their God

WORD OF ENCOURAGEMENT
(In Time of Loss)

I

Loved ones share each other's joy and pain
for loved are different and yet the same

there is an understanding from the start
that a true love is shared from the heart

when it is time to depart because a loved one
has left this life
and has moved on to yet another height
look to the light

and rely on the Greater One to carry that grief
and sorrow
only He and you really know

and then you'll see that sorrow won't last
for in time, this too shall pass

so hold fast and tight
to those good memories still vivid and bright

weeping may endure for a night but in the
morning
joy will come
with the rising of the morning sun

a new dawn, a new day to express
your appreciation for those
who truly bring you happiness

as you enter into God's rest and show your love
for life, for family, for those so dear
who help you conquer life's challenges
from year to year

II

Amazingly in the midst of it all, you'll find an
inner strength bursts through to give you the
will to continue

and strength to do all the things you must do
as you realize God is ever with you

of course our loved one shall be missed
for they can no longer be talked to
laughed with, hugged and kissed

we must sorrow not as those who have no hope
and attend to the words the good Lord wrote

death has no more sting, the grave has no victory
those who sleep in Christ shall rise again

and we shall meet them in eternity
as mortality puts on immortality

life goes on one day at a time
and each gain we make
is one more cause to celebrate

and make the most of time here on earth
to birth hope again
for absence from the body
means a new life will begin

THE SOUL OF A WOMAN

I

birthed with purpose and destiny
clothed with strength and honor
arrayed with beauty and virtue
is a woman

she gives birth to nations
to generations
for she is the strength of a nation
of her family
of her community

she is precious and priceless
her worth is far above
rubies, diamonds and gold

yet within her soul there may be
abuses, misuses and hurts untold
unheard, unresolved, unanswered

hence for ages there has been a battle
which rages within her mind
to stop her progress
and put her behind

woman understand your made up mind
cannot be stopped

no matter what shots the world has got
for the power of your made up mind
is dangerous

so you must transform your thoughts
to His thoughts about you
thoughts of peace to bring you to
an expected ending set in motion
from the beginning of time
using time to merely
take you through a process
in order for you to make progress

that's why although you may have messed up
you are not a mess up
you've had some failures
but you are not a failure
you've made mistakes
but you are not a mistake
for those things don't define
who you are

you can go as far
as you're willing to go
in spite of any opposition
or any foe

there are some things that may have happened
that were not your fault

but when you become the salt
you will wake up, rise up and walk
and tap into the greatness within

you cannot consult where you've been
to determine where you'll be
you cannot change what has been
but what will be when you determine to see
beyond your past
and set your heart to the task at hand

build up the waste places
restore the barren lands
raise up this hurting generation
and help your fellow man

when men and women get together
we are a force to be reckoned with
when we decide to uplift one another

and then there are some other
things in your life that no one really
can understand or even fulfill
for that's a space that only the
Creator can fill

II

even a man understands a woman
sees, acts and thinks different than a man
and it takes wisdom to even comprehend you
so you might as well be who you are

always strive to give your best
and be the best by far
the rest will fall in place in due time
in due season
woman you can handle it
you are here for a reason

you set the tone
you set the standard
and others must appreciate you and
meet you where you are

if you come down
before you know it
you'll be lost
and your whole life
will be all turned around

but you can stand bold and strong
when you know to whom you belong
and can truly say:
"I love me"

not because of a good job
a good education
my family
my friends
or even a man

I love me because I finally know
who I am

therefore I don't have time to be discouraged
I don't have time to be upset
I don't have time to dwell in a valley of regret
I don't have time to quit or to sit down on my
tomorrow
for my tomorrow is waiting for me
and I know it's already wonderful

I am not stuck up, I am not conceited
I just refuse to be defeated

I don't think I'm better but I know
I'm supposed to live better than that
for the fact of the matter is that
I've got the will of God on my mind
and I don't have time to be wasting time
so I've got to get with people
who are of the same mind

for you see
I'm workin' on somethin'
I'm on assignment
I'm on a mission
I've got a vision
I am going somewhere

I can't care what other people may think
or what they may say
for each day
I'm ready for a brand new day

new life
new hopes
new dreams
new songs
new places
new acquaintances
that's where I belong

I have a new mentality
I have a new mindset and I'm set
I'm on the move and I shall not be moved

everything and everybody better move
out of my way
for happy, loving and free
I'm determined to stay

III

when I remain steadfast and I pray
things will happen
kingdoms will shake
yokes will be broken
systems will quake
lives will change for the better

no matter whether or not it may seem strange
for it's not strange for a woman
to keep her eyes on the prize
until she sees purpose come to pass
with her eyes

for a man can conceive it
but it takes a woman to really receive it
and conceive it and give birth

a woman has the power to change
anything on this earth
through her conversation and lifestyle

so woman go ahead
adorn your smile
keep your joy
and rest
for the best is at hand
as a matter of fact
it's already here

throughout history
you have conquered fear
and have defied the odds
for all the world to see your victory

the price you have paid has not been in vain
or forgotten for you have gotten
this far by His grace
so keep your pace
and keep the faith and know

no challenge will be too great to overcome
no situation will be able to outrun
the power
the strength
the soul of a woman

A REFRESHING

like the destination
after the journey
like the end
after the beginning
like the evolution
after the revolution
like a brilliant morning
after the darkest night

a refreshing

like the truth revealed
after the mystery concealed
like courage
after timidity
like delight
after despair
like the clearing
after the fog

a refreshing

like tranquility
after the tempest
like confidence
after diffidence
like triumph
after the trial

like achievement
after the goal

a refreshing

like trust
after betrayal
like the genuine
after the counterfeit
like the discovery
after the search
like freedom
after bondage

a refreshing

like excellence
after mediocrity
like certainty
after incertitude
like health
after sickness
like strength
after weakness

a refreshing

like love
after hate
like prosperity
after dearth

like life
after death
like the spirit
after the body

a refreshing
a blessing
a birthing
a knowing
a flowing
an awakening into a new reality

AMERICA ON THE RISE

(September 11, 2001 changed our lives, forever. America, you are still on the rise. This poem was written during the weeks immediately following that event.)

I

America you have risen to the task
to unmask the face of terror at last

To lift up, hold up and build up
these United States

As we face up to a hidden enemy
who attacked this land of the free

But we shall not, we cannot give in
this is a battle we're resolved to win

We are a force on the move, seen and at times
unseen
keenly aware of the new kind of battle we dare wage

Writing a new page of history
a page blown upon the horizon
that will be read by generation's son

Darkness and light are mingled together
yes our lives have changed forever
still determined we are to make the world better

Engaged in transition
the face of liberty has a fresh disposition

Oh what a glorious sight!
this overdue birth of unity, collaboration

solidarity and celebration of all kindred
acquaintances, religions and ethnicities

Priorities have shifted
differences that don't even make a difference
have lifted

While we call on the gifted, talented
anointed, fearless minds
from backgrounds of all kinds for these times

Who have the expertise and know how to flow
in wisdom that we may continue to grow
and bring understanding beyond understanding

II

The future is still bright
as a nation we continue to stand tall
bold and upright

Fighting the good fight for Enduring Freedom
for justice, security, peace and joy

Among us, about us, within us
and outside our borders
while comforting those who fear and mourn
a new time, a new day, a new season is born

In the land of the free, this home of the brave
oneness must become our strongest,
our timeless enclave

One vision, one mission, a global commission
one people, one nation, a human relation

Connected by the common freedoms we act
upon and share
helping to lift humanity out of despair

In tragedy arise, in adversity arise, in challenges
we arise!
going for the gold, reclaiming the prize

Embracing the contrasts that make us strong
the wind of change has penned a new song

While we pledge allegiance
to the red, white and blue
without Almighty God we cannot make it through

Peace and be still o' raging sea
through the eyes of destiny we see
we fight for
we take hold of victory

THE VALLEY OF VISION

I

The valley of vision shows
you have seen and carried the burden
long enough. Now lift up
your eyes, arise and leave the burden
in the valley—in the gorge and forge ahead

Come up, don't look down and don't look back
for I have set you upon the canyon
upon the hill, upon the mountain
where my fountain has washed away the burden
the dirt, the soot into the valley

To reveal a healthy root never trampled
by the foot of doubt or fear
the way is clear
your time is here
was here
will be here
for it is ever settled in heaven

I have restored the true leaven in this hour
and have raised up a fruitful tree with power
branches filled with sap
dripping, feeding and giving life to many

Your demanding faith enables me
now look my son, my daughter and see

that towering, blossoming fruitful tree
touching all levels of society
unbounded by man and bound by my word
my standard
my purpose
my plan

Just ask, seek, knock and unlock
all of my glory in seasons
some reasons revealed only to you
that you may walk in love
with great faith and expectation
into a place alone and together
weathering the weather's touch
blushed by eternity's kiss

A wisp of trial, tribulation and persecution
for my name, mingled with a lifetime
of victory by the same

II

My people shall run into my arms
now sound the alarms in heaven and earth
no hurt nor harm shall breach the birth
born in time, without time, in due time
for the time has come
to see the mature ones fly or run
and the babes grow with acuity
purpose filled with rapidity
an unveiled mystery

a fluid ministry
flowing easily
breathtakingly beautiful

Acquitted and full of good works
gifts imparted into the earth
to segments of the world loss, dying
crying out to you for me
for it is you they watch, they see
while reaching out for me

Oh my son, oh my daughter
be strong and of a good courage
the wait is over
the body of burden
is dead and buried
in the valley

III

The mountain of vision shows
a blending of darkness and light
a bird taking flight followed by a flock
soaring up from the valley with joy
climbing, excelling, singing
upon the mountain a sweet song

A bird riding upon the wind
piercing the air with outstretched wings
an endless span from east to west
executing a work in rest

Its eyes red as the shed blood
fixed on the Son
following to lead
freed from the burden in the valley

A fresh olive branch in its mouth at all times
the word of God
ceaseless
ageless
endless
shameless
pure
true
and just

Massage Therapy Pressure Point #1-
The Jeep and the Elephant

Once while on a reserve in South Africa, the jeep in which I was riding stopped to let me and my fellow tourists admire a huge male elephant in the bush. To my surprise, the elephant stopped eating from a tree, turned and began to walk slowly and directly towards the jeep. As the elephant approached closer and closer, the driver of the jeep eventually backed up to let the elephant pass.

This glorious beautiful creature, the largest land mammal on earth, passed us uneventfully. It did not look to the right or to the left but kept walking straight ahead, as if it were on a mission. The elephant walked and moved like it knew its authority and how small the jeep was in comparison. If we hadn't moved out of its way, I cringe to think that it would have moved us. Now think of the greatest challenge you may be currently facing.

You are the elephant.

<u>Reflection Exercise #1</u>   Date: ___/___/___
                                     Time:_____

Based on the challenge you identified, complete the following sentence: *Today, I will overcome this challenge by taking the following actions*:

1. _____

2. _____

3. _____

Note: For your personal reference, at the top of this page record the date and time of your responses to this exercise.

INSPIRATIONAL SPA
TREATMENT II

༄༅

MOTIVATIONAL DEEP
TISSUE MASSAGE

wisdom says look deep inside
and you decide your fate
your future your state

Some people have let other people, adverse situations and negative thoughts steal their dreams. It's time to regain them, grab a hold and never let go, until your dream becomes a reality...

IT'S TIME TO DREAM AGAIN

I

Life is a manifested dream
created in stages, in phases
throughout the ages of time

it is full of changes
that cannot be ignored
for within each change
is stored a path
with winding turns
hills and valleys

those of us who dare
take the path of change
are ever changing, learning
growing and showing the
perseverance and courage
of the human spirit
when we follow through
and do not quit
but finish the path
set before us
for such a completion
is a must

I understand that to have
what I've never had
I've got to do
what I've never done
to be where I've never been
I've got to go
where I've never gone
and it is my dream
that will proceed me
and meet me at the
appointed time in time

it's time to dream again

II

For a dream is a figure
a vivid picture that speaks
to the future
and causes action
through an inner passion
which makes it come to pass

it is a prophesy
destined to be true
but can be hindered too
through hopelessness
bitterness and strife
and become deferred
a voice unheard
an unspoken word

a mere echo in the atmosphere
that no one will ever hear
but don't let that be you
let your dream
be the breakthrough

it's time to dream again

III

To stand tall bold and strong
for if you're willing to stand forever
you won't care how long

so keep a tenacity
maintain your veracity
and that bold audacity
will propel you
onward, upward and forward
step by step
by leaps and bounds

giving you the strength
to overcome mounds and mountains
of opposition
as you remain steadfast
in your position

and set your face like a flint
to conquer every challenge sent
to stop your progress

just enter into His rest
and don't give in
because it's not over
until you experience the win

it's time to dream again

IV

To hold fast and tight
no matter what others say
or what it looks like
but fight and endure
even dream bigger and
dream some more

let the substance of faith
run through your mind
develop an image
and you will find
it has a way of coming to pass
transcending the shortcuts
and failures of your past

it's time to dream again

V

To mix the seeds of your imagination
with the rain of creation
to grow a harvest of expectation

of hope, of action
of joy and satisfaction

as you realize
what you internalize
will materialize
when crystallized
in every facet of your being
your seeing will be clear
when you're not blinded by the lie
your fear

it's time to dream again

VI

Then awake, open your eyes and arise
be wise for the prize is yours
if you dare launch out into the deep
and walk on the water
where the risks are great
but the rewards are sweet
for you must see it before you be it
then you'll see it come to pass
by faith, your evidence
your assurance at last

now as you attain your dream
I give you a directive
to keep your dream

in the proper perspective
and not forget
how we've made it thus far

for we must not let
the sweat
the tears
the blood
of those who've gone before us
be forgotten or ignored by us

for they endured
to secure our gains
and now we must ensure
they remain
and continue ahead
in that vain
and not be satisfied
merely with materialism
but rise to the challenge
and change this world
turn it around
liberate those who are bound
raise up those whose hearts
are cast down

it's time to dream again

VII

But that dream
must be greater than you
and greater than me
it's all about humanity
hooking up with destiny

person by person bridging a gap
one day at a time
by sowing seeds
of time
of deeds
of substance
of self
so as to help
each generation rise
to the task

and one day
we shall look back together
and say at last
we see the fruition
thank you oh Lord
we've accomplished
our mission

it's time to dream again

THE EPISTLE

I

You are a chosen people
a chosen nation
a chosen generation
clothed in a flesh of many colors

God created you
in His own image with joy
for with the heat of His breath
He colored your skin
and He blew again
and your hair curled tight
mocking the sun's vain light

protecting your brain
as it became the progenitor
of the world's scientists, linguists, doctors
warriors, architects, artisans
masters of dance
your dynasties a marvelous microcosm

you come from a land fertile and grand
watered by the Nile and Amazon
from the snowy peaks of Kilimanjaro
to the heat of the Sahara
you made your abode

gold, silver, sapphire, onyx stone
ruby, emerald, diamond and jewels untold
you tread under your feet
and decked yourself with their opulence

elephant, lion, rhino, hippo
tiger, cheetah, hyena, wildebeest
antelope, gazelle, flamingo, zebra
and creatures too exotic to describe
vibed the plains and were tamed by your voice

so you rejoiced and danced along sandy beaches
surrounded by coral and cooled
by the translucent waters
of the Indian and Atlantic Oceans
the leaves of palm trees swaying with ease
sang you softly to sleep
like a baby rocking in her mother's bosom

II

But you were violently awakened
by pillagers in the land
sold out by your own brother man

you found yourself in strangers' hands
in strange lands
tackled, shackled
torn away from your nativity

an economic commodity
your intelligentsia, your body
used, abused and cast out
to die

so you cried
tears of shame
tears of pain
robbed of the self of yourself
by a chain

but never your true self
for to the world's surprise
it didn't surmise
the spiritual self of yourself
still survived
through prayer
and spiritual songs and hymns
shouting unto God
Oh Lawd help me!

and that He did
for against the impossible
you grew strong and multiplied
dried your teary eyes
and forced the shackles
from your ankles and hands
for the sake of your children
another generation of man

III

Now you shout
free at last!
as you peer down
the galleys of your past
and pass by your children
littering the corners of the streets
Oh God, another galley
another force to beat
out of your soul

you ask, what is this hell
that has despised my beauty
my greatness
and has forced my children
to walk through the fire
of foster care, welfare
and no care at all

as they cry and scream
reaching out for true love
only to be swept away
by the tidal wave of a system
that couldn't care less

looking in the mirror
you come to address
that the only one who can destroy you
is you

IV

Oh chosen people
oh chosen nation
oh chosen generation

wisdom says look deep inside
and you decide your fate
your future your state
for it's not too late
to hold to Jesus' hand
get real close and He'll whisper
the detailed plan
that'll take you safely
to the promised land

through the maze of genocide
back to your true destiny
rich with the fruits
of royalty

and your children
shall be restored
you shall dance again
with them and sing again
with joy

victory's song of liberty
ringing throughout eternity
never to be enslaved by anyone
or anything again

Amen and amen.

STAND

Stand in the midst of adversity
stand in the midst of uncertainty
stand in the midst of calamity

stand in the sunshine
stand in the rain
stand in the tempest
stand for your name

stand for your family
for your friends
for community

stand for your passions
fail to ration your hopes and dreams

stand for what you are believing
decreeing and praying

stand as victory in your earth
giving birth to a renewed mind

else depression, frustration, give up-tion
back up-tion, retreat-tion, depletion
weariness, tiredness and forget it-ness awaits

opportunities written in the sand
erased by waves of doubt

in the distance
a tree grows
tall and fruitful
roots deep
standing strong

TIMES ARE CHANGING

I

Times are changing, rearranging
there's a new sound around that's been found
and the reason is there is a new season
a new people on the move
who are letting God move on them

things are growing and the Lord is showing
everything you will be
no one can bar you from your destiny

everything that was, that is, that will be
is flowing together
it's time for you to get it together

are you ready for the evolution?
for the restitution?
are you ready to be the solution?
you must evolve
before you can solve anything
and make up your mind
to change your mind
for without change
there is no growth
no hope, no joy

change is a law of the universe
it's stagnation in reverse
and must start in you first

change is a sign that something
is living, giving, receiving, believing
revitalizing and realizing its potential
its greatness

nevertheless, you are where you are now
because of your choices
you have listened to either
the right or wrong voices

whoever you are hanging around
will help lift you up or bring you down
who have you let take up residence in your life?
you better think about it twice
for they are a prophesy of your future

it's time to mature and know
you may have to change
your association to reach
your destination

and perceive a challenge as merely
the opportunity to press out Divinity
it is in the center of challenge
that the Christ in you can shine through
to conquer things not of Him
and not of you

change will challenge you
to propel you to the next level
your innovative ideas

will make you a rebel
with a cause

as you go against empty laws
of tradition, religion
jargon and waste
that do not let the people truly taste
and see the goodness of God
in every area of life right now

there is a changing of the guard
old ways are dying hard
for the new will bring with it
things that sound strange
especially to them who don't
want to change

every generation brings with it
a revelation of its own identity
another ability, a new reality
a different mentality

you are a thought in eternity
to accomplish something in time
therefore time is your most valuable asset
don't just let anyone take it

time is something only fools waste
wise men and women
know how to taste and embrace
every moment, every second

every minute, every hour
and see each day
as a journey towards destiny

II

God planned your arrival
and has equipped you for survival
you are preprogrammed for success
don't dare settle for less
or become distressed by people
who are intimidated by you
by your success

rejection merely means selection

don't let the hatred, envy and jealousy
of others distract you
for what they are really saying is:
"I don't want to be me
I want to be you!"

everything you need
is on the inside of you
just tap into the grace to be you
and don't compare
for that'll wear
you out

no doubt
you require someone
in this earth to help birth

your purpose
to lead you, guide you
watch your back
redirect and direct
your steps as necessary
often to the contrary
of what you may think or feel

be for real
we always look right in our own eyes
that's why we all need someone
who is bold, strong and wise
who will not fear to say
what we need to hear

someone who is far enough
to see farther
and near enough
to see what's near

when we come near
and stop to really listen, hear and do
foolish mistakes will be avoided
situations will be aborted
that would otherwise take years
or a lifetime to make a right
out of a wrong

don't get me wrong
there are some experiences
you will have to provide
the heat needed for you
to be pure gold
or the priceless diamond
you were meant to be
shining bright enough
for you to see
in the dark

the darkest hour always comes
before the light breaks through
and then a new refreshing
an even greater blessing

know that in the dark
is where your roots are grown
the result of what
you have sown

III

Are you ready for the evolution?
are you ready to be the solution
to crime, illness, disease
poverty, depression
oppression and confusion?

or are you too busy chasing an illusion
which creates a delusion
blinding you from the truth?
those dreams always hid in your heart
from your youth

time to go back to your being
time to start seeing that you are health
you are joy, wealth, happiness, wisdom
encouragement, enlargement, abundance
and fulfillment
all of which comes out of a relationship
with Him

there will always be a counterfeit
before the true
so in spite of what you
may see or look like now
God is restoring all things
back to Himself
so get to know
your true self and
change

GET READY

Get ready to see
to move
to be
to act
to enter
to exit
to lead
to follow
to swallow
the sweetness of life
and purge the strife

Get ready to speed up
to slow down
to remember
to forget
to take hold
to let go
to flow
to know
to listen
to speak
to arise
to sleep
to stand in the balance
and weigh yourself

Get ready to stay
to leave
to inhale
to breathe
to give
to receive
to nourish
to encourage
to hope and believe
to relieve and achieve

Get ready to use time
in due time
at the right time
to be on time
for your time

Know the time is here
is now and will be
'til eternity's end without end

Get ready to be ready

COLORS

I

Time demands change
and in these changing times
it's time to reconcile and to smile
upon the diversity of ethnicity
as we embrace our destiny together

Purpose and potential must go hand in hand
from generation to generation, from man to man
so forget about the politics of rhetoric
we must now take action void of any faction

For the legislature cannot legislate
the actions necessary to get rid of hate
but we must annihilate it from the root cause
by adopting our own laws

Laws of love, laws of truth
but without Him, what's the use
for ignorance of purpose
will always lead to abuse

So I beseech you therefore hear my voice
and make the choice to stand
as one symmetry of humanness
a variety at its best

Every ethnos, every race, one component of a
greater plan
working together for the good of man
so we must understand we are stronger together
and we need each other now more than ever

For fear and death have knocked at the door
someone must answer bless God no more!
No more prejudgments based on race
we must speak life to the human race
and confront that enemy face to face

This race we can win, yes win we must
restore the joy stolen from our progenitors
restore the trust, not just in word but in deed
for all things must be restored to our seed

Indeed we shall overcome was good in its time
I hear a new song, a new rhythm, a new rhyme
being echoed in the wind,
singing we are overcoming now
and we'll stand strong to the end

II
Understand, you must first love yourself
without that truth, you can't love anyone else

I'm glad I've learned, I'm a willful manifestation
of the Creator of creation

I'm a wonderful work of art
fashioned from head to toe
yes I know I'm a bad sistah and I'm outasight
because I know who I am in Christ

I'm not arrogant but I've got to be bold
I cannot give out what I do not hold
self-assurance, self-confidence
self-love, self-respect
I must add to someone else's lack

So get into your purpose and then you'll see
the reality of what you are to do
who you are to be
and breakthrough to your prosperity

Listen to me

You are not a mistake, some incidence
the result of a merger of coincidence
you have the answer to some problems
if you have the will to solve them

Time out for foolishness, we're going somewhere
we've got to get to that place called There
and stop blaming each other for what's not right
but go to the next height by renewing your sight
you make the change to change it
you make it right!

Time is for you to make things happen
make haste, don't waste it moves so fast
step into your grace
your destiny at last

III

Let's train up our children as babes to love
and to fulfill their purpose
that's a force so strong it not only penetrates
but guards the gates to our hearts

For the future is shaped
by what we believe do and say
Don't you see? Your tomorrows
are created by your today

So today, we command hate to bow your knee
and let the minds of the people go free
Now peace arise and take your place
let the power of God's true love
liberate and destroy the hate

As we commit to be the conduit
through which unity can flow
we'll be the example to all nations
we'll be the example to follow

Massage Therapy Pressure Point #2 –
The Shuttle Bus

A friend once told me about an experience she had in college some years ago. She lived in an off-campus dorm and there was a shuttle bus that would come to the dorm to take students to the main campus. The shuttle was often crowded, so one particular day, she arrived at the pickup site approximately one hour before the shuttle was due and was the first student outside waiting.

As the minutes on her watch ticked away, another student joined her, and then another and then others until the pickup site was filled with students. The shuttle bus arrived on time. Students began to push and shove to get on the shuttle. In the push, my friend was shoved farther and farther away from the shuttle door. The bus became full and she watched in utter disbelief as the shuttle bus pulled off without her. Needless to say, she did not allow the shuttle bus to leave without her again. Now, think of a goal or dream you may have been pushed away from.

Prepare and press for your prize.

Reflection Exercise #2

Date: ___/___/___

Time: _____

Identify at least one life goal you want to accomplish and describe it below.

My life goal is:

_____

_____

_____

_____

Now, complete the following statement and fill in the blanks: *I will take the following actions to attain my goal:*

1. _____

    beginning ___/___/___ to be completed by
    ___/___/___

2. _____

    beginning ___/___/___ to be completed by
    ___/___/___

3. _____

    beginning ___/___/___ to be completed by
    ___/___/___

Point to remember: Due dates help you focus and provides your goals with a timeframe in which to manifest.

Note: For your personal reference, at the top of this page record the date and time of your responses to this exercise.

INSPIRATIONAL SPA TREATMENT III

᷾᷼

APPRECIATIVE HOT STONE MASSAGE

Be encouraged and know
these words are true
the light which shines
beams out of you

THE LIGHT

Arise shine for your light is come
A light that sees, declares, leads, guides
shows, dare goes into
the midst of unexpected change

A light that engulfs the range
surrounds and makes ready
always steady, never off
always on it to complete it

A light piercing through the darkness
annulling uncertainty, restoring clarity
discerning sincerity, preserving integrity

Correcting in measure
while treasuring, moving,
dancing, embracing, planting greatness
to grow success

A light lit by the heart and
lights every word to produce
strength on demand to stand indefinitely
to challenge boldly, to rest peacefully

A light promoting humanity
flowing together to create a new thing
a whirlwind of excellence, confidently
persuasively, tirelessly holding up a standard

Building a habitation of equity
changing what is not to what should be

A light, emanating where it will
to fulfill a set plan
in a season called Now

Be encouraged and know
these words are true
the light which shines
beams out of you

THE GIFT

A precious gift
uplifting, encouraging, inspiring
dire circumstance merely
strengthens your stance

Faithful mentor, teacher, counselor, friend
time supplies new beginnings
from an end for...

Re-creation, rejuvenation, jubilation, fascination
from year to year a renewing, a refreshing
a blessing, a reward to reword hopes, dreams
things past, unseen, unspoken, untouched
ushering in great things and even greater works

For humility's sake, wrongs are made right
darkness is made light
hurts are healed
answers revealed
mountains are made low
valleys now flow with
crystal rivers of living water

Bringing more power to being
a new anointing for seeing, believing
giving, receiving, growing
reaching, resting, rising
raising up the precious gift

Which shines, sparkles, twinkles
at every turn
a glow to attract what it would
the Son to repel what it should

Now all heaven and earth rejoices
blended voices praise the Most High God
in celebration of the precious gift
lasting years plus years plus many years to come
from generation to generation

A MOTHER'S POEM

She is a dancer
dancing to a beat that mother's hear
when they hold in their arms
one so dear who is a child

she has no time for empty thoughts
her mind being filled with dreams
of what her child can be
and will be

she dances
with outstretched arms
ready to hold, hug, lift and love
leaping over despair and hard times
for the sake of her child

her feet dance gracefully
upon soft petals of
hope, joy, faith and peace
for they are her cushion

her smile speaks a truth
that each day is new and ripe
to create what is right for her child
even when that child is grown

she dances
with the wind as her partner
they turn and turn and turn together

creating a whirlwind of praise to the most high God
which keeps her strong and shields her child

she dances
knowing there is no end to the life
that began in her womb
for that life is marked by destiny

she dances
to a song not made of soul or rock-n-roll
or rhythm and blues or rap
but made by the soulful song in her bosom
her heartbeat, a mother's beat
beating with a rhythm
of wisdom and love

God, Jesus, Holy Ghost
and His heavenly host know most
what that beat means
for they can hear it
and you can hear it too
it's unique to you
but you must be close enough

motherhood is no child's play
so mothers I salute you and say...

do your dance

THE NEXT

As you enter life's next chapter
the next word, the next sentence, the next page
is written with lessons learned
successes earned through
challenges and victories

mysteries unfold as you behold
and stand bold in the midst
the known and unknown have kissed
and their relationship has brought you into
another place, an even greater space

expanding daily with your tenacity
humanity, integrity and courage
to dare see what others don't
be where others won't
hear what others can't
say what others shant

rest in your decisions and
do not second guess
for the vision becomes clearer
with the entrance of each day

you have stay-ing power
and are rich in many ways
through the rays
of light you have imparted
to others

yes, the future is bright
now rejoice for your book is filled
with yesterdays, todays and tomorrows
sorrows overshadowed by joys
written through a severe storm of blessings

be not dismayed or swayed
by the wind or rain but remain
focused and rest in your next
for the next chapter
may be longer or shorter than the last

so select the place
settle in
choose your pen
relax and enjoy
the manuscript

THE VOW

The vow is solemn, the vow is true
　　The vow is a guarantee made between two
It's a promise, a pledge, an oath, a contract
　　It is not something to simply retract
From sunrise to sunset its payment is due
　　The contract was signed with the pledge of "I do"
Through blessings, trials, joy and pain
　　The vow still speaks, it must remain
Both parties must give at least one hundred percent
　　To make life together a time well spent
Compass your differences with the shield of God's love
　　In the midst of challenges you can rise above
The enemy hates a true covenant
　　For he knows its power is heaven sent
Pray and get the Lord's mind on how to act
　　When situations come to break the contract
Serve, respect, love, honor and yield
　　Regardless of what you may think or how you feel
The plan is set, the deal is done
　　The lives of two are miraculously one
Two souls, two hearts, two dreams, two wills
　　Merged into one flesh, one mind, one goal until
　　forever
Now arise and awaken to your greatness within
　　And let a new day of united victory begin
Your future is here, your future is now
　　Your future rests upon your daily payment of the vow

YOU

You are free to be all you want to be

for destiny is not merely of the mind

but comes to pass in due season and time

age is but one grain in eternity's sand

as you continue in His purpose and plan

while there are many things yet for you to do

be grateful for what you've accomplished
and have already come through

go forth defining your own success

better is not better until it's your best

be bold, courageous and be very strong

when the wind shifts, follow your heart's song

as you move, people may say you're unreal

be confident and know movers and
shakers make the unreal real

don't settle for less than who and what you are

you're a precious and priceless
gift and have come too far

challenges will propel you to a new level and height

giving you insight and strength to fight the good fight

the seed of your essence will grow what you need

a perpetual harvest for generations to succeed

time is your enemy, time is your friend

time serves those best who are determined to win

with integrity, empathy, grace and style

peace will distribute rest at each mile

your thirst for knowledge and answers
question the status quo

provoking thoughts and ideas force
you and others to grow

every milestone you reach announces
a continuation again

unlocking new truths beyond the horizon
where the ending never ends

every second of every minute of
every hour of every day

creation yearns, the night yawns, the day awakens

ready for another taste of

you

Massage Therapy Pressure Point #3 –
The Man and The Garden

There once was a man with a beautiful garden. Neighbors often walked by and marveled at the gorgeous blooms. As time went on, the man became busy with the affairs of life and neglected his garden. The exquisite blooms began to die and this same man was puzzled. He sought assistance from his wife to determine the problem. Upon taking a closer look through the foliage, his wife saw a weed choking the delicate flowers. She pointed out the problem to her husband who then removed the weed from the root and prevented it from ever choking his flowers again.

It did not take long for the garden to be restored to its beauty. Once again, his neighbors marveled at the splendid sight. The man was very pleased, yet his wife did not share his excitement. Her face was long and sullen. A few days later, his wife moved far away from him. Once again, the man was puzzled. Upon consulting with a friend about the matter, the friend helped the man with the garden realize that over the years, he had become a weed.

Neglect chokes relationships.

<u>Reflection Exercise #3</u>   Date: ___/___/___
                                      Time: _____

Think about at least one person in your life for whom you are grateful. Now list three actions you will take today to show or express to that person your appreciation or admiration.

1. _____

2. _____

3. _____

Note: For your personal reference, at the top of this page record the date and time of your responses to this exercise.

INSPIRATIONAL SPA
TREATMENT IV

❧❧

SELF REFLECTIVE FACIAL

I am yesterday's future
and tomorrow's finality
of today's reality

INTROSPECTION

to know myself

    I must go into myself

      to see myself

        to understand myself

          to come out of myself

          to be myself

I AM THAT I AM

I

I am the sum total of my thoughts
and thoughts of others I choose to embrace

I am the framer of my world with
words of life or death

I am the extensible manifestation
of a previous generation

I am an intellectual, a thinker, a dreamer
a being of strength might and foresight

I am a wonder of the world to behold
no complacency or normality in this mold

I am a mover, a shaker, a trailblazer, a breaker
of dead traditions of men

I am called to speak up, to speak out
to shout and tout liberation to a people counted out

I am an enemy of depression, injustice, oppression
and bad lessons of religion that fail
to empower the people
to partake of abundant life

I am a friend of truth, of light, of right
of good, of health, of wealth, of action
of dissatisfaction with the status quo

I am an anointed generation burst-
ing through ceilings
and destroying walls of containment

I am yesterday's future
and tomorrow's finality of today's reality

I am the magnification of my talk, my walk,
my surroundings, my associations, my friends

I am what I see, what I hear,
whatever I let come near me

I am victory, a triumphant winning dynamo
always moving, reaching and pressing for more
the prize without compromise

II

I am a joyful sound, a praiser, a worshipper
a spirit, a soul, a body constantly evolving
in the direction of perfection

I am beauty in motion, a marvelous work
causing commotion in heaven and earth

I am fearfully and wonderfully made
in His image, from His imagination
from the beginning a declaration of an ending
before the worlds began

I am a done deal, birthed with purpose and sealed
by the endless, limitless, timeless One
for the Father and I are one

I am that I am because of Christ
who is the very essence of my life

I am the progeny, the prophesy, a dream fulfilled
I am my ancestor's dream that could not be killed

I am progress at rest, at ease
ever growing, increasing, expanding, changing
rising, flying, where only eagles dare

I am a rare gem
somebody's ray of hope, of light
to give and impart to them words of life

I am everything I think
every single thing I believe
every solitary word I say
in the darkness of night
and the light of day

I am that I am

THE RECYCLING

armed man
unarmed boy
candy and beverage flying
unarmed boy crying out
for help
armed man pulls trigger
unarmed boy dead
gone too soon

armed man
unarmed boy
music playing
boy swaying to the sound
armed man pulls trigger
unarmed boy dead
gone too soon

armed man
unarmed boy
boy removing garbage can
approached by
strange man
armed man pulls trigger
unarmed boy dead
gone too soon

brother against brother
man against man

women doing the best
they can

promise cut short
deadly force
a first resort

a cycle recycled
over hundreds of years
despite of anguish,
heartache
heartbreak and tears

insane, inhumane
justice on trial
watched by each
generation's
man, woman and child

families, communities
cities to resurrect hope
and faith within
the cycle to be recycled
never again

touched with the feeling
of shared infirmity
the throne of grace
a necessity

greatness revealed
a nation healed
of itself
by itself
for itself

THE TAPESTRY OF LIFE

The tapestry of life is this...

To love oneself
    to love another
To know oneself
    to know another
To respect oneself
    to respect another
To free oneself
    to free another
To show oneself
    to show another
To encourage oneself
    to encourage another
To be real with oneself
    to be real with another

Woven intricately from the womb
    the tapestry of life is this...

To be oneself

LOVE

it is absolute and resolute
    not a substitute or afterthought
        for with a great price it is bought

it does not go unpaid
    it is not afraid

it sees and chooses when not to see
    hears and chooses when not to hear
        speaks and chooses when not to speak

it corrects, protects, caresses
    refreshes, blesses

heals, stands tall, kneels
    feels and feels not
        locks and unlocks the laws of life

it is real and for real
    it reveals purposes and plans
        the motives of man

it is he
    it is she
        it is earth, air and sea

it is the universe
    it must traverse
        it is love

Massage Therapy Pressure Point #4 –
Townspeople and the Snow

On a cold winter's day, snow covered the mountains, fields, crops, homes and business establishments of a town. Upon looking at the snow, one of the towns-people saw work, another person saw play, another saw a picture, another profit, another loss and another beauty. Which of the townspeople is right?

Hint: You are the snow.

How you see yourself often differs from how others perceive you. Below, list what you see as your three greatest/strongest qualities (take your time, relax and really give this some thought).

1. _____

2. _____

3. _____

Meditate on how you can use those qualities to impact someone's life for the better today. Use a blank sheet of paper to write down your ideas. Now look closely at your notes. Within them, you may have defined a need(s). This gives a hint into the type of work or business venture you may find fulfilling. Point to consider: Are you where you should be? If yes, great! If no, it may be a goal to work towards.

Note: For your personal reference, at the top of this page record the date and time of your responses to this exercise.

Afterword

❧

Upon completion of this book, you have read poems and completed four exercises comprised of three responses each. The result is that you have created twelve customized daily Inspirational Spa Treatments. Whether these treatments are applied and acted upon in twelve minutes, twelve hours, twelve days, twelve months or twelve years; they have the ability to provide focus and insight into your life, your world and how you relate to others. As your life changes, the Inspirational Spa Treatments you apply will more than likely change also, therefore revisit or rephrase them often.

In summary dear reader, from the womb of the morning we are all living poetry; epic tales intertwined with each other from an authored past, interpreted in the present to conceive a shared future. A future which reflects the tangible reality of our hopes, our goals and our dreams; and therefore who we are individually and collectively.

INSPIRATIONAL SPA

❧❧

DAILY REFLECTIONS

(30 Days)

Day 1/31

༂

When you believe in yourself, others will believe in you. When you believe in others, it is a reflection you believe in yourself.

Day 2

❧❧

Today is an investment. Determine
the type of return you want and
invest your time, mind, words, skills
and actions wisely.

Day 3

❧❧

When you tap into the greatness within, the impossible becomes possible.

Day 4

❧❧

Faith serves you. Your gifts and
talents serve others.

Day 5

❧

Genius is merely using our creative
and intellectual abilities to solve
problems.

Day 6

❧❦

High expectation is the springboard of achievement. Action is the springboard of fulfillment. Service is the springboard of a legacy.

Day 7

⚘

Be strong and very courageous. You
have the ability to turn adversity into
victory.

Day 8

❧❦

When you make the best of this day,
you make the best of yourself and the
heart of day rejoices.

Day 9

❧❧

Your thoughts and words are like medicine or a disease. The choice is yours.

Day 10

֍

Stretching your mind is good. It expands your reach.

Day 11

꩜

Greatness is a matter of thought.
Great accomplishment is a matter of
action.

Day 12

ঌৎ

Trusting the goodness within others
begins with trusting the goodness
within ourselves.

Day 13

ॐ৶

Change is a law of the universe;
it's stagnation in reverse. Be
encouraged and fear not.

Day 14

❧❧

**Stretching beyond your comfort
zone causes your world to expand to
accomplish your hopes and dreams.**

Day 15

❧❧

Each day contains joy, peace and fulfillment. Thankfulness allows you to experience them.

Day 16

❧❦

When you look into a mirror, a miracle looks back at you.

Day 17

࿔

An idea has no value if it stays in your head.

Day 18

❧❧

Whoever you are hanging around will help lift you up or bring you down.

Day 19

❧❧

Effective relationships are essential to success.

Day 20

❧

Possibility and opportunity go hand in hand.

Day 21

❧

Faith, hope and belief for something greater will eradicate disappointment.

Day 22

֍֎

Challenge is an opportunity to press
Divinity out of you.

Day 23

❦

Change will challenge you to propel
you to the next level.

Day 24

❧❧

You are the sum total of your
thoughts and the thoughts of others
you choose to embrace.

Day 25

❧

Your tomorrows are created by your today.

Day 26

❧❦

Rejection by someone means
selection by someone else.

Day 27

❧

Your made up mind is an enemy to procrastination.

Day 28

❧

You are an amazing creation. If you feel stuck or blocked, reinvent yourself.

Day 29

❧❦

Your dreams await your command.

Day 30

❧

Life is forever until it passes in
a moment. Cherish it lovingly,
embrace it fully and live it wisely.

Nettie Millard has enjoyed reading and writing poetry since she was a young child. After she began combining poetry with words of faith and sharing it with others, she received numerous requests to speak at organization and church events. The positive responses she received inspired her to produce the poetry CD *Inspiraction*, meaning "inspire to action."

A graduate of the U.S. Capitol Page School, Howard University, and Johns Hopkins University, she is an inspirational speaker and trainer currently residing in Maryland. She is the founder of NEMillard Enterprises

Inc., a consulting company specializing in personal and professional learning and development with self-awareness and self-appreciation as core values. Experience the passion of Nettie Millard's keynote presentations. Request the author to speak at your event.

Experience the passion of Nettie Millard's keynote presentations. Request the author to speak at your event.

Purchase Inspirational Spa: From the Womb of the Morning for gifts or giveaways. This book is available in paperback or ebook (Kindle).

Go to www.inspirationalspa.com.

Be on the lookout for the next book and other products in the Inspirational Spa Series.

INSPIRATIONAL SPA
A Division of NEMillard Enterprises, Inc.
P.O. Box 26561
Gwynn Oak, MD 21207
email: nettie@inspirationalspa.com

Made in the USA
San Bernardino, CA
26 August 2014